Bump! Set! Spike!

You Can Play Volleyball

by Nick Fauchald
illustrated by Ronnie Rooney

Special thanks to our advisers for their expertise:

Kinda S. Lenberg, Editor
Volleyball USA and *Coaching Volleyball*

Susan Kesselring, M.A., Literacy Educator
Rosemount–Apple Valley–Eagan (Minnesota) School District

PICTURE WINDOW BOOKS
Minneapolis, Minnesota

Editorial Director: Carol Jones
Managing Editor: Catherine Neitge
Creative Director: Keith Griffin
Editor: Jill Kalz
Story Consultant: Terry Flaherty
Designer: Joe Anderson
Page Production: Picture Window Books
The illustrations in this book were created with acrylics.

Picture Window Books
5115 Excelsior Boulevard
Suite 232
Minneapolis, MN 55416
877-845-8392
www.picturewindowbooks.com

Printed in the United States of America.

Library of Congress Cataloging-in-Publication Data
Fauchald, Nick.
Bump! set! spike! You can play volleyball / by Nick Fauchald ; illustrated by
Ronnie Rooney.
p. cm. — (Game day)
Includes bibliographical references and index.
ISBN 1-4048-1153-2 (hardcover)
1. Volleyball—Juvenile literature. I. Rooney, Ronnie, ill. II. Title.
GV1015.34.F38 2006
796.325—dc22   2005004269

Why is volleyball a great sport? Because you can play it almost anywhere. All you need is a ball, a net, and some friends. That's why volleyball is popular all around the world.

It's the first volleyball game of the season. Your team, the Aces, is excited to play. Everyone gets to the gym early to practice.

You put on your kneepads and lace up your sneakers. You stretch to loosen up your muscles. It's time to play!

4

Volleyball is played by two teams of six players—one team on each side of a tall net. Players use their hands and arms to hit a ball over the net. Each team can hit the ball no more than three times before sending it over the net.

5

Your opponents, the Spikers, show up. The referee starts the game by blowing his whistle.

The Spikers serve first. The server hits the ball over the net, but none of your teammates can get to it before it hits the ground. The Spikers score their first point.

Play starts with a serve. The server stands anywhere behind the end line and hits the ball over the net to the other team. If the server doesn't hit the ball over the net—or the ball goes over the net but out of bounds—the referee calls a fault. Then, the other team scores a point and gets to serve.

The server misses his next serve, so your team scores a point and gets the ball. The game is tied, 1–1.

"C'mon, team!" Coach shouts. "Let's make some magic now!" Mario hits a nice serve to the Spikers. The Spikers return the ball into the net, and it hits the ground. Your team is up 2–1.

Volleyball games use a scoring system called rally scoring. If the serving team fails to serve properly, or if the receiving team fails to return the ball properly, the other team wins the rally and scores a point. The object of volleyball is to be the first team to score 25 points. However, a team must win by at least two points. So, if a team is ahead 25-24, for example, it must score another point to claim the win.

A point is scored when a team lets the ball hit the ground, hits the ball out of bounds, or takes more than three hits to send the ball back over the net. No player can hit the ball twice in a row.

10

Mario misses his next serve, so the Spikers get a point and the ball. Their server sends the ball flying over the net. Your teammate Lucy isn't paying attention, and instead of hitting the ball, she catches it. The Spikers score a point and take the lead.

"You can't catch the ball or hit the net with your hands," Coach reminds your team. "That will stop the rally, and the other team will score."

11

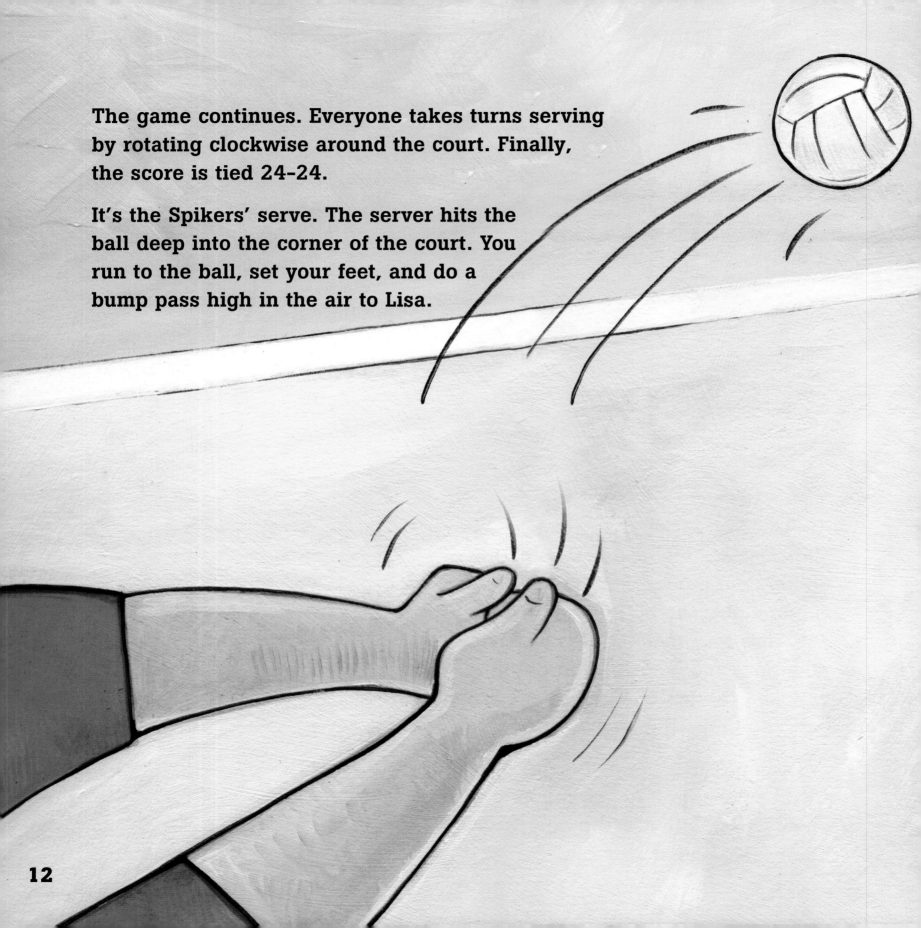

The game continues. Everyone takes turns serving by rotating clockwise around the court. Finally, the score is tied 24–24.

It's the Spikers' serve. The server hits the ball deep into the corner of the court. You run to the ball, set your feet, and do a bump pass high in the air to Lisa.

To do a bump pass, stand with your legs shoulder-width apart and knees bent. Keep your arms straight in front of you and put your hands together so your thumbs are touching. When the ball comes, let it hit the area between your wrists and elbows.

13

A set is a pass that gets the ball ready for an overhand shot called a spike. To do a set, stand underneath the ball and put your thumbs and pointer fingers together (palms up) to form a diamond. You can watch the ball through the diamond when you hit it.

Lisa sets the ball to Mark, who spikes it over the net. It looks like an easy point for the Aces, but then—THUMP!— a Spiker sends the ball back.

You race to the ball and do a dig pass to Alex, who spikes it right into the corner of the Spikers' side. Point and side-out! The score is 25–24.

"Good job, Aces!" Coach yells. "One more point is all we need!"

If a fast-moving ball is hard to reach and close to the floor, you can bend down and pop it back up with your fist or arm. This kind of hit is called a dig pass.

It's your turn to serve. You hold the ball in front of your waist and hit it with your fist. A Spiker bumps the serve back over the net to Alex.

The two most important parts of hitting a volleyball are getting to the ball early and planting your feet. Doing this will help you keep your balance and hit a straight shot. Also, don't forget to keep your eyes on the ball and watch it make contact with your hands or arms.

19

Alex bumps the ball to Mario, who sends it your way. You plant your feet, put your hands together, and bump the ball. It shoots over the net and lands just inside the end line. The Aces win, 26–24! Everyone agrees it's been a great game.

Diagram of a Volleyball Court

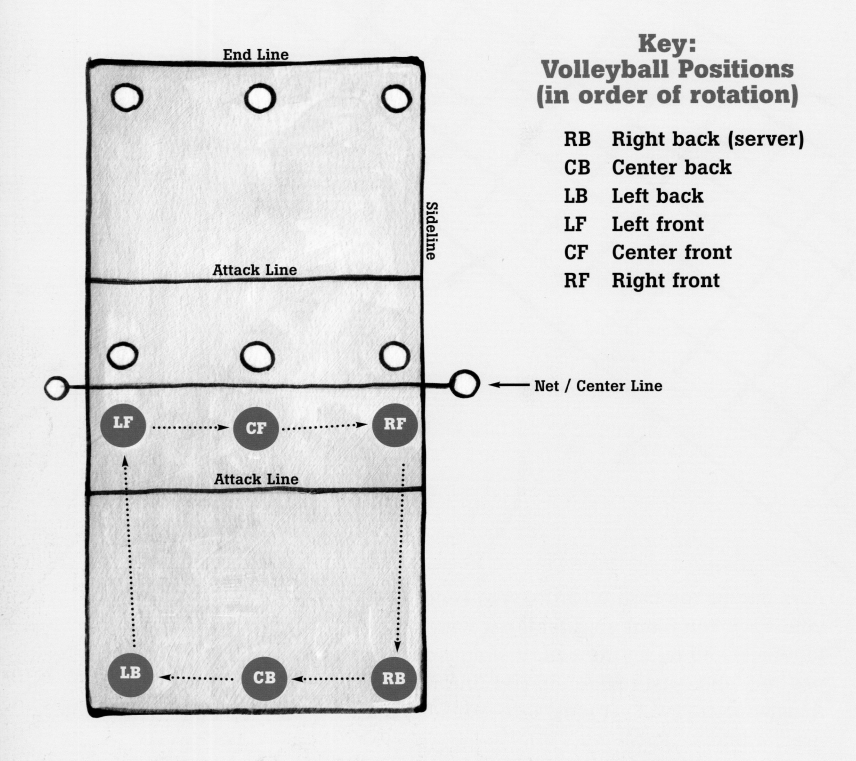

End Line

Sideline

Attack Line

Net / Center Line

LF ⋯⋯▶ CF ⋯⋯▶ RF

Attack Line

LB ◀⋯⋯ CB ◀⋯⋯ RB

Key:
Volleyball Positions
(in order of rotation)

RB   Right back (server)
CB   Center back
LB   Left back
LF   Left front
CF   Center front
RF   Right front

FUN FACTS

- William G. Morgan invented volleyball in 1895. Morgan was an instructor at a YMCA in Holyoke, Massachusetts. He wanted to create a game that would involve less physical contact than basketball, so he combined parts of tennis, basketball, and handball. He used a tennis net raised 6.5 feet (195 centimeters) above the ground and called his game "mintonette."

- American servicemen fighting overseas during WWI introduced volleyball to Europe and the rest of the world.

- Indoor and beach volleyball are now official Olympic events for men and women.

- Today, more than 800 million people in the world play volleyball at least once a week. More than 40 million of these people play in the United States.

GLOSSARY

bump—an underhand hit using joined forearms; also called a forearm pass

dig—passing a spiked or rapidly hit ball that is close to the floor

rally—a series of shots between players before a point is won

rally scoring—a scoring system in which points can be won by the receiving team or the serving team; most volleyball teams today use this system

set—a shot hit up over one's head with both hands; a set is used to prepare for a spike

side-out—the transfer of the serve, or service, when the serving team fails to score a point

spike—a hard, one-handed, overhand shot; also called a hit or attack

TO LEARN MORE

At the Library

Ditchfield, Christin. *Volleyball*. New York: Children's Press, 2003.

Jensen, Julie. *Play-by-Play Volleyball*. Minneapolis, Lerner Publications, 2001.

Sherrow, Victoria. *Volleyball*. San Diego, Calif.: Lucent Books, 2002.

On the Web

FactHound offers a safe, fun way to find Web sites related to this book. All of the sites on FactHound have been researched by our staff. *http://www.facthound.com*

1. Visit the FactHound home page.
2. Enter a search word related to this book, or type in this special code: 1404811532.
3. Click on the FETCH IT button.

Your trusty FactHound will fetch the best sites for you!

INDEX

Look for all the books in the Game Day series:

Batter Up! You Can Play Softball

Bump! Set! Spike! You Can Play Volleyball

Face Off! You Can Play Hockey

Jump Ball! You Can Play Basketball

Nice Hit! You Can Play Baseball

Score! You Can Play Soccer

Tee Off! You Can Play Golf

Touchdown! You Can Play Football